Volleyball Basics: How to Play Volleyball

ISBN-13: 978-1479210923

ISBN-10: 1479210927

VOLLEYBALL BASICS: HOW TO PLAY VOLLEYBALL

Becky Ryan

I dedicate this book to every person – who has been lucky enough to have their lives touched by the joy, excitement and sheer buzz of volleyball...

Contents

The History of Volleyball

You may be surprised to know that one of the world's most popular sports is also one of the youngest.

In spite of its youth, though, volleyball has already gone through a lot of changes that contribute to the sport's rich history.

To gain a full understanding and appreciation of the transformation this sport has gone through, it's best for you to learn about the history of volleyball.

The sport was first developed by William G. Morgan back in 1895 and given the name of Mintonette.

It was primarily created for businessmen at the YMCA chapter where he worked and promoted as a game that involved much less physical contact than other popular sports at that time.

Different aspects from a number of existing games were borrowed by Morgan in developing this new sport.

Borrowing the net from tennis, he raised the height to 6 feet and 6 inches.

He also borrowed some aspects of basketball, handball, and baseball.

The name of the game was changed to Volleyball when one spectator commented that it involved a lot of volleying.

The first official volleyball game was held at Springfield College in 1896 and this led to the sport being played at various colleges in the following years.

By 1900, the game has become so popular that a ball was especially designed for it and given the same name as the sport itself.

In the same year, the YMCA introduced Canada, the Southern Hemisphere, and the Orient to the sport.

In 1905, the sport was also brought to Cuba. This introduction of several countries to the sport marked the beginning of what's known as the Volleyball Era.

And because the sport went international very early in its development, it was able to evolve to meet the needs of different players worldwide.

The YMCA continued introducing the sport to different countries within the next ten years and in 1913, the Far Eastern Games held their first volleyball competition.

The first true evolution of the sport occurred in 1916, when the set and spike strategy was introduced in the Philippines and Filipinos developed the kill, which they referred to as "bomba."

A year later, the scoring was adjusted to end the game at 15 points from the original 21.

In 1920, the back row attack and three hits per side rules were out in place. The sport was forever changed after 1928, when official rules were finally set down.

By 1934, official referees were assigned to oversee volleyball matches.

And in the 1940s, the very first world volleyball championship was finally held, thus extending the sport's popularity even more.

It was included in the Olympic Games in 1964, thus securing its place as the world's second most played sport.

And with the increasing interest of both male and female professional players, the sport finally reached its full popularity potential in the 1980s, when it became a standard inclusion in the physical education programs of almost all elementary, high schools, colleges, and universities worldwide.

Volleyball has indeed done very well for a sport that has relatively young roots.

Basic Rules in Volleyball

Volleyball traces its origins back to the United States and although it is over a hundred years old, it's still considered as a relatively young sport, especially when compared to other popular sports around the world.

The popularity of the sport has grown not only in its country of origin, but also in a wide variety of places all over the world.

According to the latest estimates, about 46 million Americans and 800 million international players enjoy the sport, which was first developed in 1895 when William G. Morgan thought of combining a few elements of basketball, baseball, handball, and tennis into a single game.

When Morgan first developed this game, he called it Mintonette, but the name was later changed to Volleyball, which is how it's known to this day.

It was in 1896 when the first volleyball competition was held, using a basketball. It was only in 1900 that a ball was finally made especially for the sport.

It weighs about nine to ten ounces and has ball pressure of about 4.5 to 6 pounds.

Volleyball is said to be one of the most energetic of all sports. A game is typically played by two teams, with six players in each team.

Three players on each team take up positions in front of the net and the other three players take up positions at the back portion of the court. A net that's 6'6" high divides the court and each team takes one side as their playing area.

The players' hands and arms are used to send the ball over the net and into the opposing team's side of the court. The main objective of the team is to prevent the ball from falling to the ground while it's on their side of the court.

You can play volleyball indoors or outdoors and the rules of the game are fairly simple. The player positioned at the back right corner of the court is designated as the server and serves from a line known as the end line or restraining line.

You may serve the ball underhand or overhand and send it to the opposing team's side of the court.

A maximum of three hits are allowed per side, but a player is prohibited from hitting the ball in two successive hits. This is considered a foul and a point is awarded to the other team.

If two players somehow hit the ball at the same time, that's considered as one play and both players may not hit the ball in the next play. The rules of the game also prohibit making an attack on a serve.

Furthermore, only the players in front are allowed to switch positions and they can only do so after a serve has been delivered.

Just like the rules of the game, scoring is also very simple in volleyball. Rally scoring is typically used, which means a point is awarded every time the opposing team commits a foul, drops the ball, or hits the ball out of bounds.

Offensive scores are made when the defensive team commits mistakes and defensive scores are made when the offensive team commits mistakes.

A volleyball match is often played to fifteen, twenty-one, or twenty-five points.

Effective Drills

The key to gaining the best results from a training program for any sport is to customize your drills according to the specific sport that you engage in.

Regardless of how intense your training routines are, they really won't do you any good in terms of performance unless they're a perfect match to your chosen sport. This is why you really need to choose your exercises and drills very carefully.

The planning stage may, in fact, be the most important aspect of your training, as it helps you and your trainer in identifying the best and most suitable drills to include in your training program.

Here are two of the most effective drills you can use for purposes of improving your performance in the sport of volleyball:

1. Bunny Hops

Begin this drill by standing with your feet a shoulder width apart.

Next, you need to assume the squat position and then propel both of your arms backwards, right into a full swing.

As you rotate your arms forward, you should also leap forward as far as you're able to go.

Repeat the entire process as soon as you land and remember to land on both feet. It's best to go from one side of the gym to the other and then hop back to your starting point.

Take a one-minute break and then repeat the whole routine.

It's important to exercise both of your legs if you want to become a good volleyball player, particularly if your primary role in the team is to block incoming balls.

And even if you hold a different position, it never hurts to develop the ability to jump high when you're a volleyball player.

2. Bounds

The primary intention of this drill is to isolate each of your legs. Begin the drill by bounding forward using one of your legs and then landing on the other leg.

As soon as you land, you need to spring forward again as far as you can go off of the leg you just landed with.

The motion you make with this drill is similar to the one you make when you do skipping exercises.

The main difference is that, as opposed to the carefree movement of skipping, you need to place maximum effort into every single movement when you do bounds.

This is why many people also refer to this drill as power skipping.

It's only logical that drills that help you develop the ability to jump higher will offer a great deal of benefits to someone involved in a sport that requires a lot of jumping, such as volleyball.

More than just increasing the height of your vertical leap, though, it's equally important to improve your stretch reflex and reaction time.

This is why it's extremely important for you to always train at maximum intensity.

High-intensity/low-rep drills are therefore advised over low-intensity/high-rep drills where volleyball is concerned.

You need to remember as well that jump exercises without an approach are advisable for blockers, whereas jump exercises with an approach are ideal for those who are tasked to deliver kills.

Learning Volleyball

Just like in any other sport, you need to practice constantly in order to be a good player in volleyball.

If you're serious about becoming an excellent volleyball player, therefore, you'll definitely benefit from some useful tips on how you can take your game to the next level.

Following are just a few of the most helpful volleyball tips you'd do well to bear in mind the next time you hit the beach or take to the court.

1. To start with, you need to understand that volleyball is just like almost all physical sports in that it requires a considerable amount of strength and endurance training.

    This may not really be a skills tip, but it's important to prepare your body for the rigors of a volleyball game by engaging in the right stamina-building and cardiovascular activities such as jumping rope, aerobics, jogging, and resistance training. After all, you cannot truly improve your volleyball skills unless you have proper physical conditioning.

2. Passing is among the most basic volleyball skills you need to learn and master.

   Without accurate passing skills, you can be the best blocker or striker in your team, but your game will still be lacking.

   To learn how to pass accurately, your body should always be at the ready position, with your legs balanced and your arms extended.

   As you receive a serve, your arms should be straight, you should use your forearms in making contact with the ball, and you should finish the movement with your arms faced towards the target.

3. Blocking is also one of the most important volleyball skills you need to acquire in order to be successful in the sport.

   The best way of executing a successful block is by sealing the net. This is done by locking your arms with your thumbs pointed upwards.

Try to extend your arms over the net and keep your shoulders square as you make your move.

You should also try to anticipate every attack and jump straight up when you make a block.

4. Of course, you should also learn to serve the ball effectively.

Execute an underhand serve successfully by positioning the leg on your non-serving side forward.

Hold the ball at waist level, lean forward slowly, and then swing your serving arm as you drop the ball.

If you want to serve overhand, you'll have to toss the ball firmly into the air about 18 inches above your head and then shift your weight to your lead foot as you swing your serving arm to hit the ball.

Always remember to follow through when you deliver a serve.

These are just a few of the most important tips that'll help you improve your performance in the sport of volleyball.

By keeping them in mind, you'll surely be on your way to bringing your game to the next level.

Always remember that in just about any sport, the old saying that practice makes perfect still holds true.

More importantly, you should never pass up an opportunity to play a game of volleyball because you can only get better with every game you play.

Volleyball Shoes

If you seriously want to build a career as a volleyball player, then you'd do well to buy a pair of decent volleyball shoes.

The good thing about this sport is that shoes are practically the only gear you need to buy in order to do well in the game.

Compared to other sports, therefore, volleyball is pretty much inexpensive, especially since volleyball shoes aren't really that costly as well.

Aside from its affordability, the primary reason why you should buy a good pair of volleyball shoes is the fact that they're optimized specifically for the sport.

This means they're best suited to address the demands of the sport.

This type of shoe is typically packed with a host of technologies and features that can help you improve your performance in a volleyball game.

Furthermore, these shoes are generally made from materials that assist you in jumping, landing, and moving quickly, which are integral parts of volleyball.

To illustrate, one of the more popular brands of volleyball shoes uses a technology known as the gel cushioning system.

This technology helps make the shoes a lot more comfortable and adds to the support that it provides you as you play.

This cushioning system is also supposed to protect your feet from experiencing exhaustion by ensuring that they're adequately padded and kept stable at all times.

Considering the fact that volleyball players are always moving around and jumping, this is indeed an extremely advantageous feature for them and a bit of extra padding can definitely make a difference in their game.

Some brands of volleyball shoes also feature air mesh materials, which make your feet breathe a little more.

You may have noticed that sweaty feet can make a game quite uncomfortable and may even cause chafing inside your shoes.

The air mesh material can help protect you from such an experience and make you a lot more comfortable during a game, thus making you enjoy the game even more.

There are also volleyball shoes equipped with a shock-resistance feature that's very beneficial to players who regularly do the spiking for their team.

After all, when you constantly jump high into the air while playing on a hard surface, shock resistance can definitely make your landings considerably more comfortable, thus improving your endurance.

While they definitely can't provide you with the necessary skills to become good at volleyball, a good pair of volleyball shoes can surely provide you with that much-needed extra edge you won't have when using an ordinary pair of sneakers or running shoes.

The improvement in your performance resulting from wearing a good pair of volleyball shoes may be quite moderate, but the comfort and stability they provide will definitely make a huge difference in your game endurance.

If you're a serious player and you truly want to become successful in the sport of volleyball, then it would definitely be a good move for you to start shopping for the right pair of volleyball shoes as early as now.

Whatever amount you spend on these shoes will surely be well worth it.

Passing Tips

Passing is a critical skill for effective volleyball offense.

Take note that if you make a bad pass to your team's setter, the setter's chance of successfully delivering the ball to any of your hitters is significantly reduced.

As you learn more and more about the game, you'll probably notice some common mistakes players make when they pass the ball.

Of course, you'll have to make sure you avoid making those same mistakes.

Here are some tips on how you can improve your volleyball passing skills:

1. Position Your Feet Properly

Perhaps the most common mistake people make is to think that passing is exclusively about their arms.

The truth is that your passing accuracy is greatly improved when you move your feet into the proper position first before you even do anything with your arms.

You need to stay on your toes so you can easily move to the correct spot. Remember as well to keep your knees bent.

2. Pull Your Wrists Down

There are different methods for putting your hands together in preparation for making a pass and it's best for you to find the method you're most comfortable with.

More important than your chosen method is what you do with your wrists and hands. Try to pull your wrists as far down towards the floor as you can.

When you do this, you'll notice that a larger surface of your forearms is exposed, thus giving you a much flatter surface with which to pass the ball.

3. Square Up Your Arms and Hips

Another common mistake people make when passing in volleyball is to angle their arms towards the target without moving their bodies. Understandably, there are cases wherein the ball moves too quickly for you to completely get into position.

However, you should do your best to position your arms and hips such that they point straight towards your target. Doing so will greatly increase your accuracy so the setter can successfully run the offense.

4. Make Use of Your Forearms

Make sure the ball hits the middle part of your forearm when you pass it. If the ball hits your elbows, wrists, or hands, then the pass may not be as accurate as you want it to be.

Being the flattest part of your arms, the forearm naturally provides you with the greatest chance for accuracy.

This is why you need to angle your forearms towards the target and use it to direct the ball.

5. Don't Swing

Many of those who are new to the sport tend to swing their arms when they pass. Take note that this causes the ball to travel farther than you intend. Remember as well that the ball will likely have enough momentum that there's really no need to swing at it.

Your forearms should serve only to direct the ball towards the target and you should make the ball's momentum work to your advantage.

Bear these tips in mind and you'll surely be on your way to becoming a much better volleyball passer.

As a final tip, always remember to control the existing momentum instead of trying to create a new one.

Blocking Tips

One of the most important skills to learn in volleyball is blocking.

A perfectly executed block, after all, automatically translates into a point and can effectively demoralize the opposing team.

When you're just starting to learn the game, you're likely to find it a bit difficult to read the play of the opposing team and anticipate where the ball will enter your side of the court, which is essential for executing a good block.

You'd therefore do well to keep a few useful tips in mind for developing the ability to read the play on the opposite side of the net.

Perhaps the most important thing for you to remember is that you need to identify who the setters and hitters are on the opposing team before the play even begins.

Your ability to do this will make the tips discussed in this section so much more effective.

It's also important to identify who their go-to hitter is, as this makes it a lot easier for you to determine the right place to be in for a block.

The following tips will focus on helping you learn what you should be looking at and where you should position yourself, depending on the play that's developing on the other side.

Ball

The very first thing you should look at is the direction of the ball as your team delivers a serve.

Check out who makes the pass and to whom it is being passed.

Observe if the pass went where it was meant to go or if the setter had to move out of position just to get to the ball.

In case the latter occurs, your opponent will have limited offensive options and it will therefore be much easier for you to move to the right spot for a block.

Setter

The next thing you should take note of is where the other team's setter had to go in order to reach the ball for a set.

It's also a good idea to check the position of his body.

If he goes back to set the ball, then you should quickly glance at the hitters to see if they're already starting the approach. In that case, they're most likely going to run a quick attack.

Location

The moment the setter sets the ball, you should look at the location and position of the ball.

Observe if it is tight on the net, in which case it'll be much easier for you to execute a block. What's important is for you to watch the direction of the ball as it comes out of the setter's hands.

Hitter

Finally, you need to look at the hitter. If you glanced at the hitter as the setter was still moving towards the ball, then you should already have a general idea as to the type of play they're going to run.

What you need to look for at this point is the position of the hitter's body as he executes the hit. It's a good idea to line your block up with the hitter's shoulder, as this is usually the same direction in which he will hit the ball.

As long as you bear these four tips in mind, your ability to be on the right spot for a good block should improve significantly.

Serving Tips

The serve is perhaps the most critical aspect of a volleyball game.

Failure to deliver in this aspect will almost always guarantee your team's loss. In the same way, you're practically guaranteeing a win when you master the serve.

Whether you're new to the game or a professional volleyball player, it's always a good idea to brush up on your serving skills.

Towards this end, the first thing you should master is the overhand serve. Here are some tips:

1. **Body Positioning**
   Your feet, hips, and shoulders should face your intended direction for the serve. If you're right-handed, then your left foot has to be slightly in front of your right foot.

2. **Ball Positioning**
   Hold the ball at chest height in your non-serving hand. Make sure your elbow is loose and slightly bent.

3. **Arm Positioning**
   The hand and elbow of your serving arm should be bent at a 90-degree angle. Your hand should be open, your wrist locked, and your elbow at ear height. Your elbow should remain at this height throughout the serve.

4. **Tossing the Ball**
   Be sure to toss the ball 12" to 18" above your head in front of your serving shoulder. Always remember that this is the most critical part of the overhead serve.

5. **Ball Contact**
   The heel of your hand should make contact with the middle of the ball.

   Remember to keep your hand open and flat, your wrist locked, and your arm extended as you step forward. To optimize power and velocity, be sure to follow through.

In order to serve effectively in volleyball, you should also avoid these common mistakes:

1. **Poor Toss**
   The key to a good serving toss is consistency. You should therefore toss at the same height and position, aim for the same point on the ball, and strike as forcefully as you can with every serve you deliver.

2. **Loose Wrist**
   Never forget to lock your wrist when you strike the ball in a serve.

3. **Lack of Confidence**
   While practice does make perfect physically, it is your mental conditioning that can effectively increase your confidence in the game.

   It's therefore a good idea to simulate the pressures of a real game when you practice.

Of course, you need to engage in drills regularly in order to develop consistency and accuracy in your serve. Without the right drills, you're much less likely to achieve a reliable performance.

Remember that repetition effectively helps you build muscle memory, which leads to consistency and subsequently to scoring.

Needless to say, consistent scoring leads to winning games.

It's also important for you to develop an effective strategy, which can actually make or break the game for you. Strategy, after all, can effectively build your team's momentum and confidence when you execute it properly.

Finally, you need to remember that volleyball can be physically demanding and therefore requires strength, power, flexibility, and endurance.

To improve your overall performance and avoid injury, make sure you regularly engage in resistance training, which is vital in preparing you for the demands of an actual game.

Setting Tips

Setting is one of the basic volleyball skills you need to master.

Even if you're not the team's regular setter, there just may be instances when you need to take up that role so you'll have to be prepared for the eventuality.

These are the three basic principles you need to bear in mind when you set:

1. Keep Your Hands Soft Yet Strong

As the ball travels towards you, position your hands over your head with your wrists slightly cocked back.

To cushion the ball as it makes contact with your hands, flex your wrists a bit and then quickly straighten them. Be sure to use both of your hands equally when directing the ball towards your target.

Take note that there's very little difference between hands that effectively cushion the ball and hands that illegally hold the ball for too long. Breaking your wrists too much will likely get you called for a lift, thus giving your opponents a point.

Of course, your hands shouldn't be too stiff, either, since you need to take control of the ball and direct it such that it travels parallel to the net.

2. Thumbs in Your Eyes

Of course, this doesn't mean you should literally jab your eyes with your thumbs. What this means is that your thumbs should be held almost directly above your eyes when you receive the ball for a set.

To achieve the right thumb position, make sure your wrists are slightly flexed and your fingers rounded. Your thumbs should then be directed towards your face.

Take note that if you don't pull your thumbs back, then they'll likely be in the way of the ball, thus ruining your set.

As previously mentioned, your hands need to cushion the ball without holding it for too long, so you need to make sure your hands are nicely shaped into a ball. The best way to create a spherical shape with your hands, of course, is to pull your thumbs back towards your eyes.

3. Learn from Soccer

This tip may seem a bit odd, considering the fact that soccer players use their feet in handling the ball whereas volleyball players use their hands.

But, you can actually take your cue from soccer players to improve accuracy in ball positioning, particularly when they're heading the ball.

If you've developed accurate footwork and are properly positioned underneath the ball as you prepare to set, then the ball should be approaching your forehead.

This means if you move your hands away, then the ball should hit your forehead rather than the top of your head or your mouth.

Again, this isn't to say you should let the ball actually hit your forehead; it just means you have to make sure you're in the right position to successfully set the ball.

As long as you keep these three basic principles in mind, you should be well on your way towards becoming a good volleyball setter, regardless of the position you actually hold in your team.

Spiking

Ask anybody and they'll probably tell you that the best part of a volleyball game is the spiking.

About 99% of the time, a volleyball spike will come from the setter and then go to any of the five other players on the team.

The three front row players will hit the ball right next to the net whereas the two back row players need to jump from behind to hit the ball.

The various spikes that you see in a volleyball game differ in length, height, and direction, and just because the setter is faced towards a certain direction doesn't necessarily mean he won't set the ball for a back row player to hit.

Take note that the spike is typically the third ball contact a team makes, right after the pass and set.

The primary reason for using a spike is to put the ball away on the opposing team's side of the court in order to gain a point.

You should also bear in mind that spiking the volleyball isn't a single motion, but a process that begins with the completion of a motion known as the approach.

The approach is comprised of three to four steps and is followed by the jump and the actual spiking motion. When you execute a spike, remember to jump straight up into the air rather than towards the direction of the net.

When a back row player moves to spike the volleyball, the attack is known as a back row attack.

In this case, the player executing the spike needs to jump from behind the 10-foot line before they make contact with the volleyball.

After executing the spike, a back row player may then land – and usually does – close to the net or anywhere within the 10-foot line.

The good thing about this rule is that it prevents the team's best players from attacking every single ball in the front row.

Throughout the match, there are only three players who are allowed to execute a spike in front of the 10-foot line.

Ideally, you should make contact with the ball while you're at the top of your jump.

Furthermore, your arm should be fully extended above your head and slightly forward when you make contact with the ball.

If you want to hit the ball really hard, then you should take full advantage of the pike position (a quick forward contraction of your body), the arm swing, and the wrist snap.

A ball that's hit hard and straight down is typically called a bounce whereas an attack that can't be returned by your opponents and therefore earns you a point is known as a kill.

Of course, you should also learn how and where to hit the volleyball when you spike. Hitting a line spike means trying to hit the ball towards the sideline of your opponent's court.

Hitting a cross-court spike means taking the sharpest angle when hitting the ball over the net.

Other than a spike, you may also choose to execute a dump, which involves lightly coming into contact with the ball to hit it towards an open area in your opponent's side of the court.

Finally, you could push the ball into a blocker's hands to throw the ball out of bounds off of the block.

Controlling the
Pace of the Game

Have you ever participated in a volleyball game where it seemed that the pace was too fast and everything has gotten way beyond your control?

There can be times when you play volleyball that the game seems to control you.

In this case, you'll have to make a few adjustments such that you get to control the game instead of the other way around.

Here are a few tips on how you can control the pace of a volleyball game:

1. Play It Low

To give yourself time to set up the perfect play, particularly on a down ball or free ball, you'd do well to play the ball in a low yet well-balanced position.

Avoid passing the ball when it's still at shoulder level. It's better for you to take advantage of the few more inches the ball will descend to make sure you're in the best position to deliver the perfect pass to your target.

Those few seconds wherein you let the ball fall to a lower point before passing not only allow you to gain more control of your pass, but also gives your hitters enough time to prepare for their move.

These few seconds also give you control over the speed of your next play, thus helping you control the pace of the entire game as well.

2. Slow Down or Speed Up Your Pass

If you practice receiving the ball constantly, then you should develop the ability to automatically pass the ball with an arc of about four to six feet above the net straight into your setter's hands.

You may also take control of the speed of your attack by passing such that the ball will have a much higher arc to slow down the game.

This is best done when you feel that your team is having trouble establishing a rhythm.

It gives your setters enough time to think and your hitters enough time to check the court.

3. Walk Back for a Serve

Taking your time to get to serving position is advisable right after a long rally.

This effectively gives your front row hitters a much-needed breather and your other teammates a chance to catch their breath without receiving warnings for delaying the game.

Another effective strategy that achieves the same purpose is to "tie your shoelaces" just before getting up to serve.

4. Non-setters Set High

Even if you're not the team's regular setter, there may be times when you need to step in and execute a set.

In this case, you can control the pace of the game by ensuring that your knees, hips, shoulders, and forehead are properly lined up under the ball and that you get into a low position in preparation for setting a high ball to an outside hitter.

Now you should be ready to go out, establish your team's rhythm, and take full control of the pace of your game.

In every volleyball game you participate in, you should always bear in mind that the ball is in *your* hands.

Improving Your Game

If you're just starting to learn how to play volleyball, then there may be times when you get a bit frustrated about how terrible your skills are.

You may even get to a point where you start thinking you won't ever become good at the game.

If this is true, then you need to realize that you simply need to find out how to enhance your volleyball skills and speed up your skills development so you can proudly display them on your next game.

Here are some useful tips for improving your game:

1. Focus on Technique

Volleyball is one sport that's highly driven by technique. This means players with good technique are likely to prevail over those with bad technique, regardless of the level of their skills. If you're lucky, then you'll learn some very effective techniques from your volleyball coach. This is why it's advantageous to choose a coach who places special focus on improving his players' techniques.

If your coach tends to focus on other aspects of training, then you'd do well to find another player whose technique is excellent and ask him to teach you. You may also want to do some online research towards this purpose.

2. Play as Much as You Can

Just like any type of skill, your volleyball skills will likely improve if you constantly work on them. This is why it's a good idea to play anytime you can.

Whether you participate in a competition or in a friendly weekend game, you still get a chance to enhance your skills by playing as much as you can.

You could even spend some time just playing pepper with co-workers during your lunch break.

Finding as many opportunities to play an actual volleyball game helps you develop muscle memory and learn from repetition.

3. Play Beach Volleyball

Setting the ball is one of the basic volleyball skills a lot of players struggle with. It can be a bit difficult to get the ball to go where you want it to.

You may not be aware of this, but playing beach volleyball can actually help improve your setting skills. Most beach volleyball games are played two-on-two and when your opponents notice that you're not a very good setter, they'll be more likely to send the ball to your teammate so you'll be in the position to set.

The good thing about this is that it forces you to practice setting repeatedly, thus helping you quickly develop the skill.

The same principle applies if you're not very good in passing or hitting.

Since a beach volleyball game forces you to be an all-around player, it can indeed be an excellent way to develop the volleyball skills you still need to work on.

These are just a few of the things you need to bear in mind if you truly want to improve your game in volleyball.

If you seriously want to build a career as a volleyball player, then you'll have to be serious about practicing and developing all of the basic volleyball skills.

Training Tips

If you want to become a good volleyball player, then you'll need to spend a lot of time on the court.

However, you should also avoid taking the sport or your training too seriously in order to prevent burnout.

Burnout tends to happen when you become too intense about something for much too long. One day you just might find yourself getting tired of the sport you're supposed to love. When that happens, you probably won't want to practice or participate in any game anymore. A large part of your success as a volleyball player comes from your mental game, so when you no longer feel like playing, your performance is bound to suffer.

This makes it very important to avoid burnout.

Here are some tips on how to keep things interesting as you improve your game in volleyball:

1. Set Fresh Goals

Goal-setting is the necessary first step towards becoming an excellent volleyball player.

It doesn't matter if your goal has something to do with fitness or with winning championship games.

What's important is for you to make sure these goals are concrete and easily measurable so you can gauge your progress at any point.

Once you start to feel the onset of burnout, it may be a good idea to sit down and review your goals.

Ask yourself if your priorities have changed and then adjust your goals accordingly. When you do this, make sure your new goals can successfully continue to motivate you.

2. Do What You Want

To be an excellent volleyball player, you'll have to develop all-around skills. This means you have to be good at serving, passing, hitting, setting, blocking, and digging.

Most players excel at one or more of these skills, but not at all of them. This is why you need to keep practicing those skills that you know you're not very good at.

When the time comes, however, that you start experiencing burnout, it may be better to stick with the skills you enjoy practicing until you get your groove again.

For example, if you find setting drills bothersome, then you may choose not to do them for a few weeks. What's important is for you to get back to what made you love the sport in the first place.

3. Mix It Up

Cross training is a very effective way of avoiding burnout. You may not realize it, but you don't really have to play volleyball all the time in order to become a good volleyball player.

During the off-season, you may want to step out of the court and do something different, but equally interesting.

For example, you could go road biking, learn to play soccer, or simply include running in your training routine.

This works not only to keep things fresh, but also to train your different muscle groups and make you stronger.

4. Get a Change of Scenery

This tip goes hand-in-hand with mixing it up. If you're used to playing indoors, then you may want to start getting engaged in beach volleyball or simply playing at the park.

Each playing surface offers a different kind of challenge, thus requiring a different set of skills.

Regardless of which surface you prefer, the adjustments you make when you switch sceneries will surely make you a lot more versatile as a player.

Beach Volleyball
vs.
Indoor Volleyball

If you've grown to love the sport of volleyball and want to build a career in it, one of the decisions you may have to make is whether to play indoor volleyball or beach volleyball.

To help you make a better informed decision in this case, it may be helpful for you to learn the difference between these two types of volleyball game:

1. Indoor volleyball allows you to set the serve throughout the game, but in beach volleyball, you're not allowed to double contact the serve. You're allowed to pass the ball over your head, but you should make sure your hands are touching each other.

2. You're not allowed to tip the ball with an open hand. This practice, which you may be used to if you've played indoor volleyball for some time, is a definite no-no in beach volleyball. In fact, you're not allowed to do anything with an open hand.

3. You need to execute a clean set. Indoor sets tend to spin a lot, which looks quite ugly to outdoor players.

Although the referee doesn't actually count the number of spins a ball makes when you set it, you're likely to be called for doubling the ball if it spins at all. The key is to make your sets look clean to the referee.

4. In beach volleyball, you're not allowed to set a ball that's not driven hard unless the set is undeniably clean.

5. You're not allowed to side set over the net. If you do set over the net, you should do it directly in front or right behind you.

6. Beach volleyball doesn't have any rotation rules.

7. Blocking is counted among the three allowable hits in beach volleyball.

8. You're allowed to double the ball when it's driven hard, as in the case of a spike. This means that if someone spikes at you, then you can double the ball anytime.

9. This may not really be a rule, but it's definitely nice to know if you're switching from indoor to outdoor volleyball.

The ball has less pressure in beach volleyball, so you shouldn't expect them to be as pumped up as the balls used in indoor volleyball.

Don't be surprised when the ball doesn't feel as hard as you're used to the first time you play beach volleyball. You should also refrain from complaining that the ball needs more air because that's exactly the way they're supposed to be.

10. Beach volleyball typically has a smaller court than indoor volleyball. Therefore, if you're used to hitting the ball towards the back line, then you need to make some adjustments to make sure you don't hit it outside. It would be best to practice hitting straight down and using shots more in this case.

Now that you know the rules that differ between beach volleyball and indoor volleyball, you can weigh which type of game you prefer.

Better yet, you may want to try playing a few games on each type of court so you'll get a feel for the real thing and decide which one you want to focus on.

Conditioning for
Beach Volleyball

So, you've learned how to play indoor volleyball and have gotten quite good at it. You may now have decided to try your hand at beach volleyball as well.

If so, then you may as well start training for beach volleyball in preparation for the next season, particularly if you want to start joining some competitions right away.

Take note that training in this case is likely to involve more than just lifting a few dumbbells. In fact, the first thing you may have to do is learn the difference between simply working out to get fit and training for a specific sport such as beach volleyball.

Remember that when you work out for fitness and bodybuilding purposes, your focus is on executing slow and controlled reps so your muscles will grow and look better.

When you train for beach volleyball, however, your focus should be on how your muscles perform rather than how they look. Having huge muscular legs doesn't necessarily mean you can jump high enough for beach volleyball. Just take the case of bodybuilders, for example.

They have very strong legs as a result of squatting crazy amounts of weight, but that doesn't automatically mean they can jump as high as beach volleyball players with smaller legs.

We talk about jumping repeatedly because it is one of the most important things you need to train for when you decide to get into the sport of beach volleyball.

In order to gain the ability to jump high, you'll need a combination of speed and leg strength, which translate into leg power. It therefore makes a lot of sense to train for both your leg speed and leg strength.

If you're already working out your legs regularly as an indoor volleyball player, then you may no longer have to put too much focus on leg strength, as you may already have it.

When focusing on leg speed, you'll need to include plyometrics in your training routine. These exercises consist of repetitive jumping movements. That's the irony of wanting to learn how to jump higher – it can only be achieved by jumping.

This is why your training has to involve a lot of jumping. You could jump up while trying to touch a backboard or jump onto boxes.

What's important is for the height of the backboard or boxes to gradually increase so you can train your leg muscle to jump higher.

Training in this case is typically low rep/high intensity because it doesn't matter how your muscles look, but it matters a lot how they perform when you jump.

What about training with weights? Is there any difference? Yes, there is.

Primarily, you'll have to do weight training a bit differently in order to promote leg explosion.

For example, when you do squats, you'll have to go down slowly and then quickly burst back up on some sets. On other squats sets, you should go down and get back up slowly.

Remember that training the right way can effectively add a few inches to your vertical jump, which can, in turn, make a significant difference in your overall performance as a volleyball player.

Printed in Germany
by Amazon Distribution
GmbH, Leipzig